Team Building

Discover How To Easily Build & Manage Winning Teams

By Ace McCloud
Copyright © 2014

Disclaimer

The information provided in this book is designed to provide helpful information on the subjects discussed. This book is not meant to be used, nor should it be used, to diagnose or treat any medical condition. For diagnosis or treatment of any medical problem, consult your own physician. The publisher and author are not responsible for any specific health or allergy needs that may require medical supervision and are not liable for any damages or negative consequences from any treatment, action, application or preparation, to any person reading or following the information in this book. Any references included are provided for informational purposes only. Readers should be aware that any websites or links listed in this book may change.

Table of Contents

Introduction 6

Chapter 1: There's No 'I' in Team...But There's 'Me!' 9

Chapter 2: Building Your Team For Ultimate Success 16

Chapter 3: Creating a Culture of Excellence. 28

Chapter 4: Motivate, Inspire and Instill Confidence in Order to Win 33

Chapter 5: Setting Goals as a Team 39

Conclusion 43

My Other Books and Audio Books 44

Be sure to check out my website for all my Books and Audio books.

www.AcesEbooks.com

Introduction

I want to thank you and congratulate you for buying the book, "Team Building: Discover How To Build and Manage Winning Teams."

Teamwork is the building block of strong people, groups and nations. Whether you have played on a sports team, worked with a partner in school, or worked with colleagues on a big project at work, you have probably experienced working as a team at some point in your life. Teams are a great way to reach a desirable end-result in a fast, productive and often fun way. However, working as a team can often go one of two ways—either your team works well together and moves quickly toward success or your team is dysfunctional with less than ideal results.

Have you ever been on a losing team? How did it make you feel? Maybe your coach didn't pay attention to the strengths and weaknesses of the players on your team and didn't play them strategically. Maybe your partner in school was not interested in focusing on schoolwork and you didn't have the guts to speak up and take the reins. Maybe some of your colleagues felt disconnected to a project or desired end result. There are many reasons why some teams lose. It is commonly due to the fact that those teams have poor leaders.

When you are on a team that is poorly led, it can be difficult to perform at your best, especially if morale is low. You may feel disconnected from the purpose of the team. You may find it hard to trust and respect your other team members or leader. You may find that you're not even sure what your team leader wants of you. Without a solid sense of leadership, a team is much more likely to fail and no one likes to be on a losing team. On the other hand, a winning team is usually backed by a strong, solid leader who is ready to take action. A winning team has a vision, a purpose, a meaning and an established sense of trust, respect and clarity. Most winning teams are enjoyable and fun to be on.

If you have ever been a part of a not-so-great team and you are now faced with the task of leading a team of your own, look no further. This book will give you some of the best advice in the world on how to build and lead a team to victory. Don't put yourself or your teammates through the agony of defeat and disappointment. Instead, discover the secrets to team building, team development and team leadership so that you can lead your team to victory. Being a team leader is not just about leading your team from Point A to Point B—it's about inspiring and motivating a group of people to perform at their best. It's about taking control of a situation and laying out a systematic plan of action that will lead the group towards the desired goal. It's about helping others become confident so that they can excel in their place on the team.

This book contains proven steps and strategies on how to develop your current leadership skills into team building leadership skills. In this book you will discover the differences between being a leader and leading a team. You will also learn about the 6 core values of a true team leader and how you can apply them to your team for optimum results. You will also discover how to establish a culture of excellence in which everyone will want to be a part of your group and have others begging to get in. Finally, you will uncover the secrets of how to set goals as a team as opposed to setting goals in general and then you will learn the best strategies for putting everything together so that you become a great and memorable team builder and leader.

Chapter 1: There's No 'I' in Team...But There's 'Me!'

At one point in your life, you may have heard somebody joke, "There is no 'I' in team...but there's a 'me'!" This common saying is intended to be funny and sarcastic but it may actually have another, more insightful meaning. While it is true that a team consists of a group of people working together, the question is, "Who is leading those people?" That is where *you* are or will be one day—you will find yourself faced with the task of being the team leader. When it's your time to shine, you will be responsible for leading a team to success while fostering important values and ideas while managing conflicts. As a team leader, you will be everyone's "go-to" person, mentor, mediator and any other role that may come up. When you're in that position, it is up to *you* to build your team and lead it to success.

To be a great team leader, you must first have the ability to be a standalone leader. Leaders are the people who drive themselves, their organizations, and their teams to success by using several great leadership strategies to their advantage. Leaders know how to interview and recruit quality people onto their team. Leaders also know when they have to act fast. They know when they have to solve a conflict. They know that they have to plan, negotiate, practice good ethics, and inspire. Great leaders know that one of the keys to being successful is to take care of their own health and personal development to stay strong and influencing. Leaders are responsible for getting things done while working with a handful of key people. They know how to divide up tasks among team members in order to get the job done in the quickest and most efficient ways possible. They also know that they must practice good ethics, as they are responsible for everybody on the team. Nothing will bring a team down quicker than a corrupt and untrustworthy leader. Most importantly, the key job of a leader is to empower his or her team and to push them to the best of their abilities.

There is much debate as to whether leaders are born or made. While there is no direct answer, logic says that anybody can become a leader. The difference is in one's actions and behaviors. For example, anybody can be given the title "manager," but to be a successful manager, you must tap into the leader within. What matters most is that without leaders, teams would not likely get very far. Without a leader, teams might not even exist.

When you're a leader, you can help develop others into great team players, as your leadership skills will help you be a great team player yourself. Team leaders are responsible for several things when it comes to managing a team. There are 5 stages of team development, known as the forming, storming, norming, performing, and disbanding stages. Each stage is an indicator of progress for a given team.

During each stage, it is up to the leader to take action, which will bring the group through these 5 stages.

The forming stage is usually when the members of a team meet each other for the first time. If nobody has ever worked with each other before, there are usually negative emotions going around, such as fear, distrust, and discomfort. During this stage, it is the responsibility of the team leader to bring down the team's level of discomfort. You can do this by finding common ground on which the team can come together. You can also play some "ice-breaker" games to help everyone get to know each other.

The storming stage is usually when the team transitions from a regular group of people into the actual team, meaning they start to learn from one another. However, this stage can also cause some conflict. You may find that your team consists of people who have large egos or who don't agree with others ideas. As a leader, it is your responsibility to serve as the mediator in this stage. You can encourage everyone to be open about their thoughts and feelings. If any conflicts arise, it is your job to work with the conflicting parties to come up with a solution so that the team can move on to the next stage.

The norming stage usually happens once the team gets out of the forming stage. You will know that your team has reached this stage when the team begins to get along and make progress toward the end goal. As a leader, you will probably not have to do much during this stage except work alongside your team and encourage them.

Then there is the performing stage. The norming stage will transition into the performing stage as your team begins to seriously make progress. Your team will be in synergy with each other and they will work through any obstacles or challenges that come their way. During this stage, it is up to you to delegate tasks in a strategic fashion. You may also give feedback to team members so that they can improve on their work. Ultimately, you should motivate your team and reward and/or appreciate them during this stage. At this point, you should know your team very well, so you should be able to tell what will work and what won't work with your team members along with what types of rewards and motivations work best for them.

Finally, the team will move into the disbanding stage. This is when the team has reached the goal and is ready to move on to another goal. Sometimes, this means creating new teams with new groups of people. The only risk with this stage is that some team members may be opposed to change, which could heighten the chance of negative emotions. As a leader, you are responsible for encouraging change.

Throughout these 5 stages of team development, you will also have to foster and develop core values. These values can help turn your team into a productive powerhouse as they are geared towards success and progress. They are easy to remember because they all start with the letter "C."

The first core value that you must establish as a leader is communication. As the leader, you must communicate to your team about their roles and give them feedback as to how they are doing. Without communication, your team will be unable to make progress.

The second core value is control. As the leader, it is up to you to have control over your team. You must make sure that the team has control over the work and that you are holding them accountable for their responsibilities.

The third core value is creativity. As the leader, it is up to you to encourage and foster creativity. Teams that are creative often have more opportunities and ideas to work with. Creativity can also enhance the communication of the group if everyone shares their ideas. If you would like to know more about how to be more creative be sure to check out my book: [Creativity: Discover How To Unlock Your Creative Genius And Release The Power Within](#).

The fourth core value is competence. As the leader, you must make sure that your team is able to complete the tasks given to them. If not, you might need to rethink or retrain them.

The fifth core value is collaboration. Collaboration is a powerful resource when used correctly. As the leader, it is up to you to promote friendly collaboration and to mediate any conflicts that may arise. Collaboration can also go hand-in-hand with creativity.

The sixth core value is clarity. As the leader, it is up to you to make sure that your team understands the concept of teamwork as well as the goal they are working towards.

The seventh value is commitment. A team that is committed works well together and is in sync with each other. As the leader, it is up to you to encourage commitment as one of the core values of the team.

Finally, to be a great team leader, you must build and practice good ethics. As the leader, your team will follow you, so it is crucial to be moral and ethical. This can help strengthen the values of your team and encourage better teamwork. Your team members will be more likely to feel a sense of security and protection knowing that they are all appreciated and treated fairly. It is important to remember that diversity can actually foster more ideas than a team of people who are all very similar. Try to avoid favoritism or singling out and be sure to treat everyone on the team as equally as possible. For more advanced information on being an incredible leader, be sure to check out my book: <u>Leadership: The Top 100 Best Ways To Be A Great Leader</u>.

Now that you know a little more about what it takes to be a great leader and team leader, it's time to discover the top strategies for building your team.

Chapter 2: Building Your Team For Ultimate Success

Building your team is a process. As you learned in Chapter 1, team development usually goes through 5 stages. In this chapter we will go a little more in-depth about team development and what you can do to build a successful, ethical and positive winning team.

Recruiting. One of the most important things when it comes to building your team is finding the best and most qualified people to be on it. A team succeeds or fails based on the leader, the strategy and the quality of the people making up the team. If you are in a position to build your own team, be sure to do it wisely. It's very easy to have one poor performing team member bring down the morale and productivity of the team. Be sure to do a thorough interview for new members, asking all the important questions pertaining to the position all while trying to find someone who is eager to perform and work hard! If you find that someone is just not pulling their weight, as the leader it is your responsibility to either side line or replace ineffective team members with those that may be more qualified or are more professional. The top recruiters in the world get paid millions of dollars per year in order to acquire the best talent available for their teams. Take your time and build your team by finding the best, most qualified and most enthusiastic people to fill your ranks!

Building Good Relationships. Having strong, healthy relationships is important in all aspects of life, but especially when it comes to teamwork. The stronger the relationships are among you and your team, as well as between other team members can be the difference between success and failure. Teams that foster strong, positive relationships tend to be more productive than teams with clashing, negative relationships. When a team has a strong bond with each other, the members are more likely to work above and beyond to produce an amazing end result. The stronger the relationships, the less room there is for negative, uncertain feelings or attitudes.

When it comes to encouraging positive team relationships, you should look back to some of your leadership core values. Communicate your expectations and requirements to each team member so that everyone is on the same page. When team members know their responsibilities, they can work together to be fast and efficient. Don't forget to communicate how important it is to build positive relationships with each other. Communicating with your team can help them build upon their strengths, therefore boosting <u>confidence</u>, which is always an important ingredient for healthy relationships. Encourage the team members to recognize the strengths of each other.

As a leader, you can build the relationships of your team by setting a good example. Set the tone for your project and your team will follow along. As long as you stay consistent, your team will likely get along well, knowing that everyone is working hard towards the same goal. Try to always listen to the concerns of your team members so that you can build a solid foundation of trust. If possible, encourage good relationships outside of the team. Also, be sure to celebrate accomplishments, no matter how big or small. You should also encourage good communication, clarity, commitment, and collaboration. In just a few short pages, you will learn about some great strategies which you can use to encourage strong relationships among your team members.

Building Positive Attitudes. Having a positive attitude is the difference between being a winner and a loser. If you go through life with a negative attitude, you will likely see negative outcomes. The same goes for your team. The more positive your team is toward reaching the end goal, the more productive and successful they are likely to be. Having a negative attitude will not get you or your team very far.

Encouraging a positive attitude can be easy, especially if you are a naturally optimistic, goals-oriented leader. However, upon further inspection, you will see that there are several stages in which you can approach attitude. They are known as the civility, respectability and likeability attitudes.

First, as the leader, you must solve any conflicts that arise during the storming stage. Before you can set your team up for a positive attitude, you have to make sure that nobody is bumping heads or trying to put the other team players down. This is where your ethics and morale skills come in. Once you've resolved any conflicts that may have arisen, you can then focus on building a team with a great attitude.

Civility is a good attitude at its most basic form. With this attitude, you don't have to like or get along with your team members, but you do need to act in a manner in which you tolerate the other team members and work together towards the end result as best as you all can. This attitude tries to minimize conflicts or arguments in an attempt to get your project over with as quickly and painlessly as possible. While this attitude is good to have in the early stages of your team development, it is important for the team leader to move the team out of this attitude stage early on. The key here is to try and build *strong* relationships and attitudes so that team members actually get along, work well together and like each other.

Respectability and likeability are two types of attitudes that are much more efficient for building great teams. Respectability is a stage of attitude in which you respect somebody because of certain values or traits that they hold. For example, you may respect somebody because they have a master's degree or because they are always on time, or because they hold a prestigious position. There are many great values and traits that bring people much respect in the workplace. Let's say that you have a team member who is always on time with things, no matter what—you can count on them. As the leader, you can assign that person to write up the report that goes with your project. You will know that the person will deliver it on time and your team members will also see that, thus establishing a sense of trust and respect. Assign appropriate tasks to all of your team members based on their strengths, abilities, and qualifications. By doing this, you can avoid hitting people with work that might not be challenging enough or that may be too overwhelming for them. This will help you create a positive team attitude and everyone will feel respected.

Once you've organized your team and assigned them with the best tasks that suit their talents, they will more than likely start to work well together. Your team will be under control, doing the things they do best, and making progress. Out of this often comes likeability. When your team is doing tasks that they find comfortable and are good at, they are much more likely to open up to each other, get along, and even develop friendships, all of which can help boost the overall spirit of the team.

Building Good Ethics. Building strong team ethics is important for the daily functioning of your team. As you know, negative emotions such as fear and distrust often arise during the early formation of most teams. As a leader, it is important for you to set workplace ethics and follow them. If you do not lead by example, you risk your team members not taking the ethics policy seriously. While it is up to you to write up the ethics policy of your team, there are many values you can add to it. Here are some examples:

- Integrity
- Equality
- Respect
- Responsibility
- Diversity
- Courage
- Dependability

A really good idea is to write up a mission statement for your team. When a mission statement is in place, your team members have a core ideology to attach themselves too. For example, if you're passionate about diversity, wouldn't you want to work with a team that fosters diversity? If you can create a team that is connected to your core team values, you can bet that the team will work much harder to succeed! You can make the team mission statement as unique as possible. The more unique it is, the more people it is likely to attract. The more passion you can encourage, the more production you are likely to get in return.

For some really awesome tips on how to write a team mission statement, check out this YouTube video by SamplesHelp's channel, How to Write Team Mission Statements.

Building A Good Environment. Environment can mean two different things. First, your environment can mean your surroundings. Research shows that the messier your environment is, the less likely you are to get things done. This is why it is important to consider where you will hold your team meetings. The most common place to hold meetings are in conference rooms or empty classrooms, as they contain the least amount of distractions. If you are holding a virtual meeting, it is best to sit in a quiet, well-lit room with as few distractions as possible. Some other ways to label your overall environment include:—attitude, ethics, moral, actions, behaviors, etc. In this sense, your environment can directly affect your team morale.

As a team leader, it is important to have good control over how you handle the overall environment of your team. This can make or break whether your team gets things done or stays stuck on step one. If you can create an incredible environment, people are much happier and motivated! Here are some great strategies you can use to ensure a creative, collaborative, and controlled team environment:

Offer Coaching. If a team member needs help sharpening their skills or understanding something, offer to be their coach as well as their leader. Coaching another team member can help strengthen relationships and boost the overall confidence of the team member. Your team member could also then pass on the knowledge to the rest of the group along with some praise for the leader. If team members Know that they can rely on you for extra help, coaching can really strengthen the environment of your team. There's a reason why the best coaches in the world get paid millions upon millions of dollars a year!

Be Specific With Goals. Goals sound so easy to set but the reality is that the best goals are specific and well-thought. If you told your team that the goal was to create a computer program, you might actually be leaving them in the dust. They will be faced with many questions, such as, "What kind of computer program? What platform?" A better goal would be one that is more defined, such as, "Create a bookkeeping computer program for the Windows platform that will automatically update itself." With that goal, your team will know what kind of computer program they will need to make on a specific platform and they will know what exactly you want the program to do. I have also found an incredible computer program for making goals. Ever since I started using it my productivity increased noticeably. If you're interested in one of the best goal setting programs in the world that emails your goals to you daily then check out: Goals On Track.

Clearly Define Roles. Without roles, your team may become lost. As the leader, it is your responsibility to delegate tasks and assign roles to your team. Going with the last example of creating a computer program, defining roles can look something like this:

Your team consists of Mike, John, and Susie. Mike has a bachelor's degree in graphic design. John has 20 years' worth of programming experience. Susie knows a lot of people and is really good at networking and marketing. So if they were going to design a Window's computer program that featured automatically updating bookkeeping software, you could put Mike in charge of the visual aesthetics, John in charge of writing the code, and Susie in charge of marketing the program to everybody she can reach in the world of accounting. At that point, the team will have the goal and they will have their roles so that they can jump on the project and start working on it right away. In the end, you will have a nice-looking, well-designed program in the hands of those who can benefit the most from it.

Encourage New Ideas. Think back to Chapter 1, when you learned why creativity is so important. Many people associate creativity with things like writing, painting, or music, but creativity can and often does extend into the workplace. To create a positive team environment, always encourage new, creative ideas. Most people have unique ways of looking at things, so it is important to listen to all and any ideas. You might think you have the best idea for the project to run efficiently, but then you may discover that John, who is looking at the problem from a different angle, has an even better idea.

Offer Incentives. There is some debate as to whether incentives can boost the development of a team. Some say that rewards and incentives serve as good motivation and others believe they can actually be a motivation killer. Luckily, there is an effective way to utilize rewards and incentives in a team setting. If you have a team that will likely disband after the project is complete, don't give out long-term incentives. Also, if you give a high-performing team member a raise, they will likely begin to take that raise for granted later on. Instead, give out bonuses or one-time incentives. This way, your team members will be more likely to stay motivated and passionate.

I personally have found that incentives work great when utilized properly! When I was younger and working at Wells Fargo, the manager offered all the salesmen and women the opportunity to win a red hand squeeze ball for the person who got the most sales that day. I put it into high gear and beat out everyone, winning the ball. Now the ball wasn't even worth that much and the company made hundreds or thousands off of the sales I produced, but just the symbol of being the winner is very enticing! I still have that red ball to this day and enjoy squeezing it to strengthen my forearms and hands every so often, and I am always reminded of the day that I beat out the whole office quite convincingly! Besides bonuses, think of trophies and other sorts of items that can be very motivating!

Gently Hand Out Constructive Criticism. Constructive criticism is important for helping your team members improve. However, you should deliver it in a gentle, respectful way if you want it to be effective. If you come off as an authority and deliver constructive criticism with a negative attitude, your team members may feel offended. Approach your team members on a friendly yet firm level and let them know what you expect of them.

If you're not sure how to approach somebody for constructive criticism, check out this YouTube video by OfficeArrow.com How to Give Constructive Criticism for tips.

Recognize Individuals and The Team. If you're looking for a great motivator, you could see what happens when you make your team and each member feel important. Always recognize both the team as a whole and each member for his or her important contributions, hard work, dedication, and anything else that they've brought to the group. You will also feel great about yourself knowing that you are encouraging a strong team.

Chapter 3: Creating a Culture of Excellence

One of the most important steps in creating and leading an effective team is knowing the difference between setting team goals and setting team expectations. Team goals are the end results that the team is working together to achieve. Team expectations are more like a set of standards that your team will follow while working towards the big picture. Setting team expectations can help create a culture of excellence, make your best members even better, and combat the hindering effects of whining and complaining. Many businesses and organizations have their own set of standards printed in their employee handbook. However, it is up to you, the leader, to ensure that everyone is following those standards.

The standards that your team must follow ultimately end up becoming your team's culture. A workplace culture is defined as a group of people who share the same values, assumptions, and attitudes. Creating a culture is a great way to control your team's behavior. It also serves as a learning experience and promotes interaction, all of which are necessary for a strong team to thrive.

Work Smart, Not Hard. Time is precious and invaluable. Many teams are usually faced with a deadline to reach their goal. To make the most out of that time frame, it is important that you establish a "work smart, not hard" culture. There is no exact way to follow this formula. It all depends on your team, the project, and the resources on hand. Here is one basic example so that you understand this better: let's say that your team got started on the project but halfway through, they discovered that they were going about the project the wrong way. However, the team already had done most of the research and started building the project. Instead of throwing everything away and starting from scratch, the team could brainstorm to see how they could salvage the work already done and use it optimally for completion of the updated project.

Self-Belief. If your team members do not establish a sense of self-belief, it is likely that the end goal will come out to be weak or underdeveloped. In Chapter 4, you will learn some excellent techniques for instilling Confidence and Motivation in your team members. However, it is important that some of their confidence and motivation is self-driven. That being said, it is important for you to encourage a "steel sharpens steel" culture. Let your team members encourage and learn from one another. Always give off a positive attitude and never ridicule anyone, especially in front of the entire team; otherwise your team members may actually become discouraged.

Communication. Communication is important in teams, otherwise nobody would be able to work together. However, communication is more than just having your team members talk to each other. Communication is being able to understand each other and convey messages in order to get things done. A team with a high level of communication in their culture is generally much happier and work together better. Encourage your team to take notice of the way their colleagues communicate. Some people are better with nonverbal communication than verbal communication. Understanding this can help your team members feel more safe and respected.

Embrace Change. Change is something that many people are opposed to at first. While change can be scary, it is important to encourage your team to embrace change as a part of their culture. When your team learns to embrace change, many doors of opportunity open and new ideas can spring forth that can take the team farther than they'd ever imagined. Encourage them not to be afraid of risk-taking and new ideas. Remind them that change is important in life and that sometimes it happens involuntarily. Some of the most successful people on the planet and throughout history are those that have been able to adapt to change quickly using intelligent strategies and a lot of enthusiasm!

Use Humor. Research shows that adding a little humor to life can make a huge difference. Don't be afraid to laugh with your team and have a little fun. This can usually de-stress everyone and help them lighten up and refresh themselves for the next step in the project. Team members who know that they can work in a lighthearted environment will be more likely to want to be a part of the team.

Establish an Open-Door Policy. Team members who feel that their opinions are valued are more likely to be happy and productive workers. Don't be a stranger to your team members and encourage them to talk to you. This can help establish a culture of trust and mutual respect. Welcome criticism as an opportunity to get better and be sure to let team members know that they can trust and confide in you.

Discourage Whining and Complaining. Whining and complaining never gets you anything but wasted time and annoyed teammates. Spend some time instilling a sense of self-belief and a "can do" attitude in your team. Discourage whining, complaining, and any other negative, time-consuming behavior. Winners never whine or complain—they keep on striving, despite any obstacles or challenges they may face! Don't let your team become trumped by failure—instead, teach them to embrace it. Whatever you do… Don't let that rotten apple spoil the bunch! As a team leader, if someone is just plain old sucking or just bringing down the team consistently, be sure to try and replace them with someone who is trying to win and succeed!

Share Responsibility. Create a culture in which everyone shares responsibility. This way, you can reduce the chances of your team members bumping heads with each other or not equally playing their part. When your team knows that they can count on each other to work equally towards the end goal, it can make your work environment a much happier place. I don't even want to think about the amount of offices and other team environments in the last ten years that have been filled with the whining and gossip of people complaining that "so and so doesn't pull their weight!" Try and avoid this at all costs!

Work With the Future In Mind. Finally, always work with the future in mind. Leaders who think a few steps ahead are often those who cross the finish line first. Thinking ahead of the game can help you stay on top of trends, think of great ideas first, and be the first to capture your audience. Teaching this strategy to your team can give you twice as much of an advantage.

All in all, create a culture that you would want to work in. If there is anything about your leadership or teamwork style that you find questionable, take a good look at it and ask yourself if you would want to be in the shoes of your team members. Creating a culture of excellence can be a great way to boost ideas while keeping your team productive and happy.

Chapter 4: Motivate, Inspire and Instill Confidence in Order to Win

Motivating and Inspiring Your Team For Ultimate Confidence

One great way to motivate and inspire your team for ultimate confidence is to get everyone together and work on some challenging games. These types of games often allow your team members to practice their communication, collaboration, and creativity skills with each other, which can help strengthen relationships, foster new ideas, and allow your team members to feel great about themselves. Playing these challenging games can encourage a fun and positive workplace environment.

One way you can be sure that these games instill confidence in your team members is to encourage the right behavior. Let your team know to be active listeners and always to be positive toward each other while saying things like, "awesome idea!" Encourage everyone to work together. Do not allow anyone to ridicule or exclude each other. Always promote laughter, as that can usually spread a positive attitude.

Games That Instill Confidence

Game #1: Have Your Cake and Eat It, Too. For this game, the goal is to break the team up into pairs or individually and bake a cake that represents either the organization or the goal that the team is working towards. At the end, you can judge which cake is the best representation. This game is a fun way to challenge the team's creativity and collaboration skills as well as bond over some tasty desserts.

Game #2: 2 Truths and a Lie. This challenge is a good icebreaker game for when your team is in the forming stage. For this challenge, each team member sits in a circle and thinks of two truths and one lie about themselves. Everyone takes turn stating 3 things and the rest of the team has to guess which statement is false. This game is an effective way for everyone to build trust and become comfortable around each other as well as practice their critical thinking skills.

Game #3: Break the Knot. For this game, have each team member stand in a circle with their shoulders touching. Then have them grab the hand of somebody across from them (but not the person right next to them). Once everyone's hands are together, challenge the team to untangle themselves without letting go of each other. This challenging game helps encourage teamwork skills such as communication, cooperation and problem solving.

Game #5: Building Trust. This activity can help build trust among team members. You will need a blindfold and some creative thinking skills. For this challenge, one team member gets blindfolded and has to walk from point A to point B, which can vary. I have seen teams do this while walking down a set of stairs or just simply walking to a point of interest. You could spread some objects out in the room to serve as obstacles. The team members who are not blindfolded have to direct the blindfolded team member by saying things such as "walk 2 steps left, go straight, stop, etc." Another great challenge for establishing trust is to do the "trust fall," in which team member's pair up and take turns gently falling into each other, trusting that they will be caught.

Game #6: Building a Positive Attitude. This activity requires the pairing of team members. It is meant to sharpen feelings of confidence and positive attitudes. For this challenge, each partner takes turns telling the other partner about one memorable bad event that happened to them. The first time they tell about the event, they can focus on the negative aspects of it. Then they have to retell the event but while focusing on the positive things that came out of it. The partner who is listening can help pick out the good that came out of it.

Game #7: Idea Killers. This challenge focuses on motivating team members to only think positively. Before the team begins to brainstorm and move into productivity, make a list of negative words and phrases and post it in a visible area. The rule for this challenge is that anytime a team member uses one of those words or phrases they have to put a quarter in a jar. At the end of the project, your team will be in the habit of only using positive words and you can use the money to buy the team lunch.

Game #8: Writing a Mission Statement. This challenge allows team members to feel passion and inspiration. Earlier in this book you learned about how important it is to have a mission statement. For this activity, you can have team members write out their own mission statements as to what they think is important when it comes to teamwork. At the end, let everybody read their mission statement out loud. This challenge can help team members find common ground with each other and it works <u>creativity skills</u>.

Game #9: Encouragement Jumper. This is a fun activity that is a good way to let team members eliminate stress, laugh and practice motivational encouragement. The object of the game is to place a piece of paper high up on a wall and let each member run and jump to place a mark on the paper. After that, he or she is told to try again and aim higher. You can optionally hand out rewards for this. The only catch is the team member isn't allowed to use a chair or other device—they have to go by the encouragement of the rest of the team.

Game #10: Letter Writing. This fun and relaxing challenge is a great way to let each team member motivate each other through their genuine opinions. The object of this challenge is to break the team into pairs and have each member write a letter to their partner, highlighting their best traits, characteristics, and accomplishments. They are only allowed to write about good, positive things. Then let each partner exchange letters and read about themselves.

For some more great icebreaker tips and ideas, check out this YouTube video by tldgxqx19: Team Building Tips: Ideas For Team Building Icebreakers.

Winning With Incentives

Everybody is different and will be motivated by different rewards. While a paycheck is the most typical "reward" for hard work, it can easily be taken for granted. Most people work to earn their paycheck so that they can keep up with the cost of living. Therefore, their paycheck doesn't come off as much of a reward... more like a necessity. Some organizations reward employees on a "pay for performance" scale, but there is much debate as to whether or not that is effective either. The true rewards are usually never associated with money.

When you offer incentives for your employees, it can say several things about yourself as a leader. First, your employees will appreciate the fact that you appreciate them. Secondly, when newer employees see that you offer incentives, it can sometimes make them work harder to win. Finally, it shows your team that you care about them. They will feel a connection with you.

Incentives can range from simple to complex. Some people can feel like a winner from a simple pat on the back or compliment. Other people love getting physical reminders of their hard work, like a certificate that they can frame and hang up. Incentives can be a bit more deep. For example, you could give out designated parking spots, take people out to lunch, throw them parties, buy them a personally engraved gold medal, trophy, or plaque or buy them something they've been needing, or you could even offer them a free week of vacation. The ideas are endless and ultimately up to you. Another good idea is to give out some gift cards. It is just as important to think back to your ethics. Always try to let everyone have a chance at earning an award. If you keep rewarding the same person, it can possibly lead to some conflicts. A good idea would be to try and implement each reward into something that encourages teamwork.

Chapter 5: Setting Goals as a Team

All throughout this book, you have heard about setting goals. As a team leader, what does that exactly mean? Goal-setting is a crucial skill for being successful in life overall but when it comes to setting goals as a team; it is possible to look at it in a different light. The main purpose of a goal is to get your team from Point A to Point B—from the forming stage to the disbanding stage. Setting team goals can help you get there fast and in an efficient, productive manner. The time to set team goals is during the norming stage, once everyone is comfortable with each other and ready to focus.

When you set personal goals, you are the only person who has a say in brainstorming, outlining and achieving them. When you're leading a team, it is important to give all team members a chance to help set the goals. By doing this you can also help to get everybody on board for maximum productivity. The key is to work with your team to set short-term and long-term goals. Aim for a mixture of 3 to 5 goals, but don't overwhelm yourselves. Review each goal as a team to make sure it is specific and realistic.

As you work with your team to set goals, be sure to apply the strategies and techniques that you have learned in this book so far. A good idea is to outline this step using all of the six C's.

Collaboration. Team goal-setting means that everyone gets the opportunity to suggest ideas and make comments on the team's potential goal list. Sometimes the best ideas come from two or more people putting their heads together, so encourage everyone to suggest at least one idea. A good idea is to have your team get together and brainstorm ideas using a white board or a piece of paper.

Communication. Communicate your expectations of the team with the end- result in mind. When your team knows what you're leading them into, it can help them come up with relevant ideas. For example, if the overall goal of the team is to write a book on public policy, let them know so that nobody puts out ideas on writing a book for a different topic. Encourage your team to actively listen to everyone's suggestions and ideas.

Control. Once you and your team have narrowed your goals down to a mixture of 3 to 5 short-term and long-term goals, evaluate each one together and make sure that each one is realistic. If you and your team find that one goal is too unrealistic or unattainable, go back and think of some more ideas. There is nothing that kills productivity more than trying to achieve an unrealistic goal. Make sure that you and your team have a good sense of control over each goal.

Creativity. How creative is each goal? Can you or any one of your team members come up with a creative approach to tackling each goal? Can anyone come up with a way to reach each goal faster? Open up your meeting to creative ideas and see what you can come up with. How does each goal relate to the mission statement of your team? Remember how important creativity is when it comes to working together to get ahead.

Clarity. Once you and your team have a good sense of your goals and how you will achieve them, be clear on your expectations. Break down each goal and delegate tasks to those who can best get the job done. Be specific when discussing your expectations with your team and encourage them to talk to you if they do not understand any part of the task. It is always a good idea to start off a goal with the phrase: "I will easily..."

Commitment. Finally, make sure that you and your team are committed to achieving each goal with the end-result in mind. <u>Motivate</u> your team to be passionate about tackling each goal. If you find that one or more of your team members are not committed, you may want to consider playing some icebreaker games to warm everyone up or talk with them privately to come up with a solution. You can also encourage them to think about how nice it would be to win at the desired task and become the champions. It is always much more enjoyable to show up to a large event as the recent champions. I have personally had the privilege to be on quite a large amount of winning teams, and I can tell you from firsthand experience it is quite enjoyable to win! You only live once! You only have this one chance to truly make your mark on this planet. Let your voice be heard and lead your team to Glorious Victory!!

Conclusion

Leading a team is hard work but if done with the right strategies in mind, it can be a successful, rewarding experience. You learned about team development and the different stages that teams go through as well as the 6 "C"s of effective team management. You now know what it takes to distinguish yourself from being a leader to a team leader. You now also have a better idea of how to create an effective culture while leading your team to excellence. Hopefully you will be able to try out some of those icebreakers from Chapter 4 and make some good memories. Don't forget to take everything you've learned and put it all together when planning out your goals.

All in all, I hope this book was able to help you to better master your ability to lead a team. The next step is to practice the 6 "C"s, even if you're not in charge of a team yet. Apply them to your current leadership position and sharpen them so that they're ready to go when you do become a team leader! Remember to try and always do what is best for the team so that everyone wins! As the leader, you need to make the tough and intelligent decisions that will guide your team to great joy and happiness!

Finally, if you discovered at least one thing that has helped you or that you think would be beneficial to someone else, be sure to take a few seconds to easily post a quick positive review. As an author, your positive feedback is desperately needed. Your highly valuable five star reviews are like a river of golden joy flowing through a sunny forest of mighty trees and beautiful flowers! *To do your good deed in making the world a better place by helping others with your valuable insight, just leave a nice review.*

My Other Books and Audio Books
www.AcesEbooks.com

Business & Finance Books

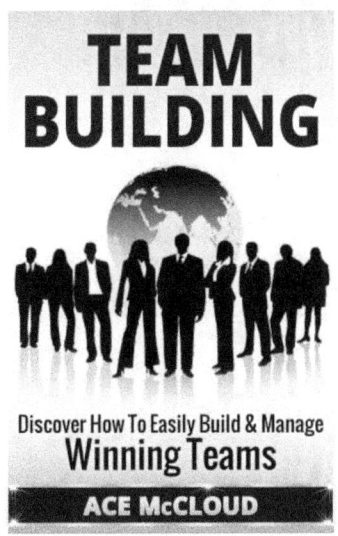

Peak Performance Books

Be sure to check out my audio books as well!

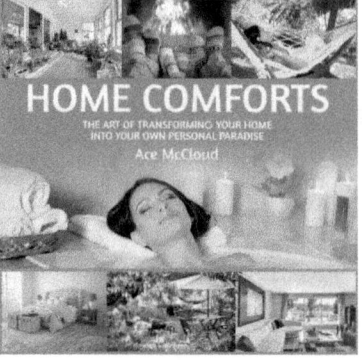

Check out my website at: www.AcesEbooks.com for a complete list of all of my books and high quality audio books. I enjoy bringing you the best knowledge in the world and wish you the best in using this information to make your journey through life better and more enjoyable! **Best of luck to you!**

www.ingramcontent.com/pod-product-compliance
Lightning Source LLC
LaVergne TN
LVHW081517060526
838200LV00005B/198